STEP-UP
and make it
HAPPEN

MJAE DUREZA

INDIA • SINGAPORE • MALAYSIA

ISBN 979-8-89026-785-6

How Often Do You Ask Yourself,

Can I Do it?

Can I Try again?

Is it Really Possible?

Will I Achieve it?

When Can I Do it?

*The answer is **NOW!***

We'll Take it a Step Further and Re-fuel Your MINDSET.

CONTENTS

PREFACE

Frequently, we find ourselves on the brink of giving up what we dream of accomplishing because of unanticipated obstacles. Often, we forget the initial spark when we realize our dreams for the first time.

Do you still remember how excited you were that day when you decided that you wanted to achieve something? However, it's common for that feeling of excitement to turn into discouragement and unmotivated over time. Due to many external factors, most of them is no longer in our hands.

When decisions are based on emotion, they are tricky and most often lead us into anxiety and discouragement.

Thus, how many of us get back up and finish our unfinished tasks?

Grit and tenacity are some of the characteristics we must possess to succeed.

Meanwhile, our beliefs are influenced by the people we follow and those who influence our thoughts. These are some of the things we need to examine and revalidate to get back on track in achieving our desired goals.

Now, are you ready to start?

Let's step up and make things happen.

ACKNOWLEDGEMENTS

My father used to say, "Play now, pay later" or "Pay now, play later"; either way, you'll do both. Thus, always opt for delayed gratification over instant gratification.

To my dad Jose Polanco Ret. Police Colonel (PCOL) and my mom Judith Provido who have been my strength and inspiration while exploring my life's purpose. Your support and encouragement allowed me to discover my inner strength, capabilities, and potential. Your love, Dens, James and Xavier, inspire me to move forward despite the challenges.

To my mentors and friends, Dr. Jesus Torres, Dr. Junifer Abatayo and Dr. Rodalyn Asenas, who always challenge my thoughts and direct me towards my dreams.

To the CFC community leaders and friends who constantly reminding me that life is more than just achieving my dreams, and that it's important to always keep my feet on the ground.

To my fellow educators who inspire me to always see the bright side of things, for all the challenges that taught me how vital it is to work together for a common goal.

And to you my wonderful readers,

Regardless of how big or small your dreams are in life, this book can provide many insights that can help you discover your hidden potential and enable you to finally achieve your dreams.

This book is for you.

INTRODUCTION

This book contains many valuable lessons and realizations that can help you uncover your potential. The power to create an impact lies within you. The differences that make you who you are, who you are capable of being, and who you are destined to be, make you unique and uniquely capable of contributing to your family, community, and society.

It is crucial to acknowledge that some situations are beyond your control, such as things that happen in your environment. It includes weather conditions, your neighbors' reactions, your classmates' opinions, and those who believe you cannot succeed.

Henceforth, you can control your mindset and how you see yourself. The focus of your attention must be on something you can control. That is your MINDSET.

Throughout this book, you will discover many topics that can give you greater control over your thoughts, feelings, and actions.

In this book, the author intends for you to discover your inner self and capabilities. As you come to realize your personal goals, you are progressing towards achieving them. Whatever they may be.

It is significant to discover your inmost mind.

The famous Abraham Lincoln said, "The best way to predict the future is to create it." That is possible with the help of this book.

It is your unique personality that sets you apart from others. Ultimately, you are what you choose to become. And it's time to embrace your unique differences and discover your hidden abilities. Let's go and get started.

Let the JOURNEY Begin!

TOPIC 1

DETERMINATION

"I believed success is achieved by ordinary people with extraordinary determination"

– Ziglar, Z.

It was a rainy afternoon when Samantha's class was over. She has, at last, completed her drawing plates ready for submission. She wrapped it up, put it in the drawing tube, and was ready to go.

Darkness was all over the place as the heavy rain soaked the ground in water. It was difficult for her and the rest of the students to travel back home. As it was after 8 pm, there was no transportation available due to flooding, and it was raining.

Suddenly, one of her classmates shouted, "Samantha, *let's walk home, we can't stay here."* Her classmate was a working student who juggled his schedule in the morning with studies in the afternoon as a student. He's one of Samantha's closest friends. Excitedly, without hesitation, Samantha agreed, and the rest of her classmates joined them.

Fearlessly, they began walking in the flooded area, and the water level was up to their knees. Their shoes and uniform got wet and cold. It is common to experience this kind of flooding during the rainy season in the university belt.

There is no turning back since they are already soaked in water. After walking for more than an hour, in wet clothes, in the pouring rain, and almost wearing-out shoes from the rain. Samantha and her friends complained about their situation. Most of them are tired and hungry.

They stopped multiple times to rest. Samantha and her classmates have no choice but to walk until they reach their destination, "home."

"There are better starters than me, but I'm a strong finisher."

– Bolt, U.

In that experience, they learned two very significant lessons: first, think twice before walking on something, as there's no turning back; second, keep walking despite the challenges, such as coldness, hunger, and tired muscles until you reach your destination.

Determination has no limit. Once you start something, it is a MUST to complete it. As the saying goes, it's not how you start things, but how you FINISH them. That's what MATTERS.

"It's not how you start, but it's how you finish"

– Phelps, M.

Recovering from last night's experience, Samantha and her classmate welcomed the day full of excitement and enthusiasm. They have this favorite professor who inspires them to be successful draftsmen/draftswomen someday. Mr. Ford has taught at the university for some time. At the snap of a finger, he can complete a perspective drawing using a marker on the whiteboard.

Meanwhile, AutoCAD during that time was only offered at the highest level. During the first year, you will be taught how to use a T-square, technical pens made by either (Staedtler, or Rotring), a compass, LeRoy for lettering, and other materials you will need for technical drawing. Taking part in this kind of training helps them become the finest draftsmen they can be.

Imagine if they all continued until they completed the course. However, some of Samantha's classmates drop out in the middle of the term, and the difficulty of the subjects is one of the factors. Needless to say, quitting should not be in the vocabulary of someone DETERMINED to graduate. *After so many humps and bumps, sleepless nights, group study activities, and other academic undertakings, finally they completed their technical course in Graphics Technology.*

Empowered, Samantha's journey doesn't end there. Being part of the student council and at the same time elected as chairwoman for the commission of student elections (COMSELEC), she discovered her passion is teaching.

To fulfill this, she takes a ladderized course. During this time, Samantha worked in the BPO industry. She decided to study in the morning and work at night. Determined, she enrolled in the program. Her work normally starts at 9 pm and ends at 6 am – After the shift, she goes straight to the university. Her class would start 8 am and end at 1 pm. After that, she traveled for an hour or so. She used this time to eat lunch and complete her tasks for her subjects. Most of the time, she slept on the bus because of exhaustion, mentally and physically. Multiple times, the driver woke her up since she was the only passenger left on the bus. She usually reached home at 3 pm, then rested until 7 pm. She's been in that situation for 2 semesters until she decided to join evening classes.

Finally, Samantha completed her course and was awarded the most Outstanding Teacher demonstrator upon graduation. Aside from that, she was also promoted to Team Lead (supervisor) at her work, handling 18 technical support agents at a young age; most of whom are way older than her. Despite that, she leads the team and motivates them to excel.

Many people, like Samantha, juggle their schedules in order to reach their ambitions, despite the challenges they face. They refuse to give up until they accomplished their desired goals in life.

PERSONAL APPLICATION/REFLECTION:

Now let me ask you, what's your **GOAL/S** in life?

1.1   What do you want to achieve?

Write it down here:

____

____

____

____

____

____

____

1.2   How do you want to achieve it?

____

____

____

____

____

____

____

____

____

1.3   What are the possible problems you might encounter
       along the way:?

a. ____

    ____

b. _______________________________________

____

c. _______________________________________

____

d. _______________________________________

____

1.4   How you will resolve it?

a. _______________________________________

____

b. _______________________________________

____

c. _______________________________________

____

d. _______________________________________

____

TOPIC 2

EXCEPTIONAL THINKING

"The exceptional life depends not on working harder, but on different, even opposite, actions from habit and the crowd"

– R.W. Emerson

The next topic will be about being exceptional in the way that you think. The subject of DETERMINATION was discussed previously, and how Samantha and her classmates overcame many obstacles along the way. They worked and completed their academic journey at the same time. Eventually, they achieved their goals.

Note that their struggles and challenges are only temporary, as they were sustained to cross over from being students to becoming exceptional leaders.

Samantha and her classmates possess a clear vision of life, and they refuse to give up despite challenges. Their goals are clear and solid. No matter what difficulties they face along the way, they never stop striving. They continue until they reach their final destination.

A xenial relationship between individuals who add value to each other can be considered exceptional. Through this kind of connection, they uplifted one another. Everyone has the potential to fulfill their dreams when fueled by hope and determination.

Take a look at those groups of individuals who aim for greatness. For example, a professional organization or a group of athletes aiming for success. What do they do? They meet regularly to monitor their progress. With that process, it is not disputed that they can achieve their goal/s.

One famous actor says success is not always about greatness. It's about consistency. Consistent and diligent work leads to success. Creating the possibility of reaching your dreams is not easy. It will require your focus and energy to carry on and move forward despite the challenges.

When the pandemic hits the entire world, people realize that everything they plan ahead of time can be halted with the snap of a finger.

Many have experienced losses, such as businesses, and loved ones, and even mental health seems to be a problem for many. People don't have the option, but by soaking themselves in front of their television, watching the news, or series to ease the boredom experience. Those past years were struggles for all.

However, with the right mindset, many people still use these setbacks to their advantage. Despite the fact that most people prefer to relax over pursuing their dreams, those who pursue them never give up.

A person who strives for greatness develops his or her current knowledge, and they are the ones who are exemplifying the virtues of exceptional thinking. Those who venture into online businesses, they learned about e-commerce and transformed their venture into a platform with increased visibility and more customers due to its nature.

It is undeniable that embedded ingenuity, positive thinking can take you to another dimension. By choosing to feed your minds with constructive things, you are more likely to succeed.

Persistent determination is the key to overcoming challenges along the way. You may feel deteriorated when you suddenly thrown into trials that test your tenacity and resilience.

Thus, an exceptional individual will never succumb to thoughts of failures and heartache. As a result, that person will continue to rise and grow into the person he/she wants to be.

Majority of people tend to overlook the importance of day-to-day performance and its long-term effects. What must take into consideration are the small choices you choose to acquire daily.

Rarely people do observe how most successful individuals struggle to prepare themselves for daily tasks that affect their success in the future.

What J. Maxwell profoundly explains is that SUCCESS is a Journey, not a destination. The action of stimulating that impetus daily is already a significant advantage in the face of an unseen opportunity.

In Samantha's case, her daily temporal struggle with preparing in advance for a long commute using public transportation just to avoid traffic was admirable. She must pass this challenge daily, whether there's favorable weather or adverse.

Human beings are however bound to many aspects of negativity. Thus, ignoring those negative thoughts can be considered exceptional thinking too. Many people tend to dwell on those unfavorable voices, which paralyze them from moving forward. The ability to outsmart negative thoughts and transform them into positive ones can have a profound impact on everyone's humdrum.

"When we realize the true meaning of life, ourselves, and the world around us that is true wisdom".

– Socrates

Normalizing that positive response would result in a great outcome over time.

Being exceptional doesn't mean that you have to be part of something BIG. It is about making small gestures that can add value to you personally and in return to other people. Upon waking up in the morning, your mindset will determine the course of your day, and the remainder of the activities you will be engaging in.

Furthermore, legislators' laws bring orderliness to the citizens, thereby developing a sense of unity not just physically, emotionally, but also psychologically and concerning one another. Having this kind of governance can be called exceptional thinking.

Meanwhile, what are the small gestures/actions you can do daily that could spark changes?

Examples of small gestures you can DO to prepare your day.

Make ready the things you need in the morning or the night before you sleep. I.e., the clothes you will be wearing, shoes, socks, your bag for school, homework, etc.

Plan your activities for the day; You can create a timetable for your class or daily tasks. You may include your daily readings (15 - 30 minutes) and also, engage in physical activities such as playing badminton, table tennis, basketball, walking, running, yoga, etc. The most important thing is to stick to your schedule.

At the end of the day, assess your planned activities if you have accomplished them or if perhaps you need to exert more effort. Then start doing it all over again.

PERSONAL APPLICATION/REFLECTION:

2.1   What are the small choices you made beforehand that have made a significant impact on your life?

____

____

____

____

____

____

____

____

2.2   Which small actions you can make to DEVELOP yourself?

Mentally? b.Emotionally? c.Physically? d.Socially?

a. _______________________________________

____

b. _______________________________________

____

c. _______________________________________

____

d. _______________________________________

____

TOPIC 3

BEING FEARLESS

*"The only thing stopping you is **fear**, and the only thing that will get you past it is **courage**. What you do with your life isn't up to your parents, your boss, or your spouse. It's up to **you** and you alone. "*

– Pavlina, S.

In ancient times, a person was fearless when they exterminated multiple opponents on the battlefield. The Colosseum is the memorial to that once upon a time, people had to fight until their last breath before they were considered FEARLESS.

Courageous is the name of the game. Without it, it is impossible to conquer combat. The opponent must be destroyed to impede the attack. That was from time immemorial. The days of bloodshed battles are gone. People have become more educated, and now value life more than ever. Things can be solved diplomatically without violence.

The emerging generation of educated people has shifted this bloody scenario into a more diplomatic era where everyone is considered equal.

This time our battlefield is the MIND. What you feed your mind influences and affects your thinking. This is your combat zone. Furthermore, how you use the time that you have daily can be considered your field of operations.

The art of adapting constructive thinking can be practiced. This is accomplished by exposing yourselves to good books, videos, and other source material that could enrich your minds.

Knowing that what comes out of you when you are squeezed is what is inside of you.

Raising the level of your accepted customs can have a tremendous impact on your daily productivity. That is to make your daily habits productive.

On top of that, you'll learn how to laugh when things don't turn out as you planned. Don't take yourself too seriously. It is evident that people who practice failing forward become more successful in their chosen endeavors.

One of the leading authors J. Maxwell once said, "Failing forward is the ability to get back up after being knocked down, learn from our mistakes, and then move forward in a better direction."

Fearlessness is exemplified by a constructive disposition in the way you think about what you are capable of becoming.

By consuming daily episodes and drama series on social media platforms, which has become the norm for many since the beginning of the pandemic, this action can cause the undiscovered potential to be deprived of reality, which can quickly lead to an uncultivated or undiscovered capability.

That hidden talents and skills that are buried in a person's being are left uncharted. Whether you like it or not, what you feed your mind shapes your perceptions, and your perceptions shape your realities. Seeing these fundamentals at the onset of a person's realization can support rational thinking to its advantage.

Being fearless doesn't mean you are not scared. Of course, you do, you FEEL it. However, you come forward and say to yourself, SELF we can do this, and that is COURAGE. Having courage is similar to being fearless.

The capacity to move forward despite failures, rejections, and heartaches is called being FEARLESS. When you think of giving up because it's too challenging to continue, times when you are afraid to stand in the crowd to speak up; when you fight for the rights of others despite fear, that's the time you are building your muscles of being fearless; You see, many are already valiant, in their own ways.

A person's ability to win after defeat signals their ability to be stronger than their perception of themselves.

"A true test of character isn't how you are on your best days, but how you act on your worst days"

– unknown

PERSONAL APPLICATION/REFLECTION:

3.1   What are your fears?

____

____

____

____

____

____

3.2   What are the things you need to do to overcome them?

____

____

____

____

____

3.3   What is your favorite quote/philosophy that inspires you to move forward despite your challenges?

____

____

____

____

____

____

3.4 Create a framework that will support your daily journey toward success?

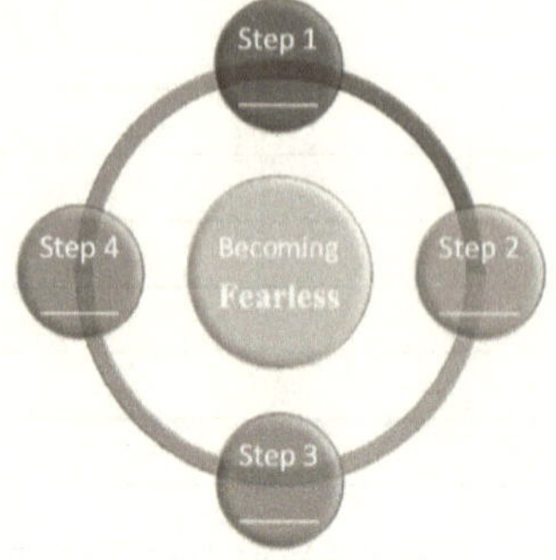

Fearless (Framework)

Step 1

____

____

Step 2

____

____

Step 3

____

____

Step 4

____

____

TOPIC 4

INDIVIDUALITY MATTERS

"To be yourself in a world that is constantly trying to make you something else is the greatest accomplishment"

– Emerson, R.W.

You see, you are already courageous in your own way. Being able to win after defeat is a sign that you are stronger than you can imagine. The word individual is defined as an entity that exists independently of others. It is a distinct quality with its own needs, goals, rights, and obligations.

Everyone possesses different qualities that make their existence unique. People comprised of different qualities that make them complete. In a family, some were born "introverts" who prefer to be alone most of the time, and others are "extroverts" who like to mingle with other people. The mother may have a sanguine nature, while the father is melancholic, and their children might possess both. This makes the family unique and complete. (For a clearer understanding of personality types, you will discover them at the end of this topic).

Imitating others can cause havoc in your personal life. Discovering your unique characteristics can help you understand your personality. Being yourself is more valuable than being a copy.

As the oldest in the family, Samantha possesses a distinct personality that makes her excel especially in sports. Her friends, however, enjoy other activities.

Samantha shows enthusiasm for track and field and the long jump. When she was in grade school, she was one of the representatives for the track and field and long jump competitions. Her kinesthetic learning style was very visible at a young age. Her participation in the event introduced her to athletes from different schools, most of whom were taller than her.

In the final match, she ran alongside a giant. This athlete's height seems to be half of hers. For every step the athlete took, Samantha took two steps. Imagine the tenacity and stamina she must exert during that match.

There were around 15 players in that event and Samantha got the third place as one of the smallest and youngest competitors. That time, she and the rest of her schoolmates took a chance to win the inter-school meet.

Although she was not selected to compete in the district meet, at least she represented her school. That kind of experience took her sense of discipline and courage to another level.

Nowadays the society has changed tremendously due to technology and accessibility. Most young people are openly exposed to so much social media engagement. They are either influencers or being influenced.

However, when you gather a deeper understanding of your own selves through affirmation, self-actualization, self-discovery, and deeper knowledge of one-self, you can free yourself from imitating others.

As you learn more about your unique qualities and characteristics, you will realize that indeed, you are special, unique, and irreplaceable. Your identity differs from your parents', siblings', relatives', and friends'.

Validating the results of your personality test with friends and family members can help you understand your unique characteristics. This can influence your thoughts about becoming the person you are supposed to be.

Develop a sense of responsibility to live according to your discovered qualities and characteristics.

You must discover your hidden potential, actualize your skills, and live up to your life purpose.

Conclusively, a Choleric is one of four temperaments described by the Greek philosopher/physician Hippocrates as the basis of human personality traits and characteristics.

PERSONAL APPLICATION/REFLECTION:

4.1   Are you an introvert or an extrovert?

____

____

____

____

4.2 What are your hidden qualities? How can you contribute to your own and others' success?

____

____

____

____

4.3   In what ways can you influence the youth? To discover the potential they possess?

____

____

____

____

4.4   What qualities do you want to develop and why?

____

____

____

4.5   What's your personality type?

____

____

____

____

The 4 personality types are:

1. Melancholic (earth)
2. Choleric (fire)
3. Sanguine (air)
4. Phlegmatic (water)

Choleric

"Ruling, Dominant" type

Strengths
-ambitious
-passionate
-leader-like
-focused
-efficient
-practical
-good at planning
-good at problem solving
-confident
-motivating
-a delegator
-usually right
-great in an emergency

Weaknesses
-agressive
-domineering
-inflexible
-impatient
-rude and tactless
-argumentative
-unable to relax
-uncomfortable around emotion
-low on empathy
-discouraged by failures
-too busy for people
-intolerant
-a leader who demands loyalty

Roles:
Leaders
Producers
Builders

Fire

Melancholic

Earth

Strengths
-thoughtful
-considerate
-cautious
-organized
-an excessive planner
-schedule oriented
-detailed
-highly creative in poetry, art and invention
-independent
-good at preventing problems

Weaknesses
-obsessive
-too cautious
-prone to depression
-prone to moodiness
-perfectionistic
-pessimistic
-difficult to please
-deeply affected by tragedy
-a person with tunnel vision
-sometimes a procrastinator
-discontent with themselves and others
-prone to play the martyr

Roles:
Artists
Musicians
Inventors
Philosophers
Doctors

"Avoiding" type

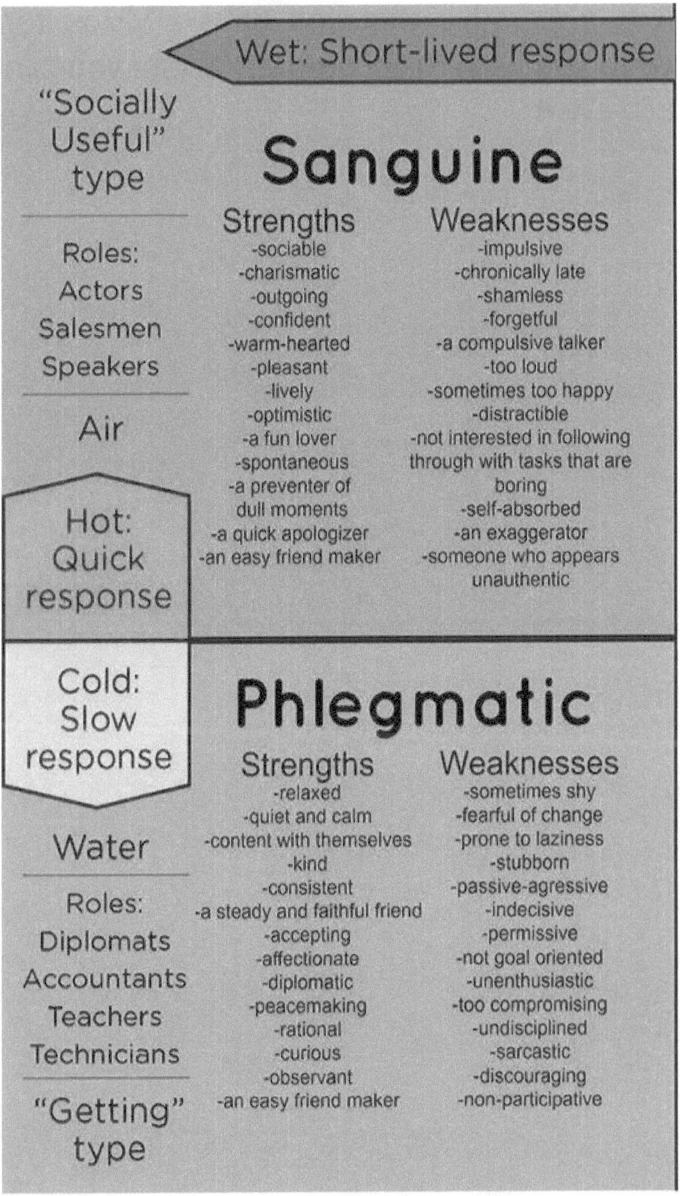

Wet: Short-lived response

"Socially Useful" type

Roles:
Actors
Salesmen
Speakers

Air

Hot:
Quick
response

Sanguine

Strengths
-sociable
-charismatic
-outgoing
-confident
-warm-hearted
-pleasant
-lively
-optimistic
-a fun lover
-spontaneous
-a preventer of dull moments
-a quick apologizer
-an easy friend maker

Weaknesses
-impulsive
-chronically late
-shamless
-forgetful
-a compulsive talker
-too loud
-sometimes too happy
-distractible
-not interested in following through with tasks that are boring
-self-absorbed
-an exaggerator
-someone who appears unauthentic

Cold:
Slow
response

Water

Roles:
Diplomats
Accountants
Teachers
Technicians

"Getting" type

Phlegmatic

Strengths
-relaxed
-quiet and calm
-content with themselves
-kind
-consistent
-a steady and faithful friend
-accepting
-affectionate
-diplomatic
-peacemaking
-rational
-curious
-observant
-an easy friend maker

Weaknesses
-sometimes shy
-fearful of change
-prone to laziness
-stubborn
-passive-agressive
-indecisive
-permissive
-not goal oriented
-unenthusiastic
-too compromising
-undisciplined
-sarcastic
-discouraging
-non-participative

It is imperative that you have a vision for what you wish to accomplish before you can achieve it.

TOPIC 5

ASPIRING GREATNESS

"Don't aspire to make a living, aspire to make a difference"

– Washington, D.

As you continue to discover your inner strength and potential, let's move on and discuss your aspirations.

The thing to remember is that to achieve your goals, it does not matter whether they are big or small, what matters is that you have the desire and drive to succeed.

Whatever goal you are working towards, your small daily actions will have a major impact in the long run.

With a relentless focus on reaching that goal, that desire will grow even stronger. Having a vision of something you can accomplish is a good thing. You must stick to that. As the journey unfolds, you will encounter challenges, so be prepared to handle them. It does not matter how big or small the goal is, as long as you focus on reaching it.

Previously, in Samantha's story, you learned her personality. She is choleric, strong-willed, decisive, goal-oriented, and output-oriented person. One summer, Samantha needs extra money to pay for this activity at a summer youth camp.

Her father was a strict cop whose aim was for Samantha, the eldest in the family to succeed in her personal life. He also wanted her to pay attention to his instructions while under his care.

At the beginning of the semester during Samantha's first year at university, her father transported her to and from university. Like any father, he was very protective of her.

He would support anything related to her academic studies, except extracurricular activities. Samantha was having trouble convincing her father to support this endeavor. Fortunately, she maintains a positive relationship with her father. She can appeal to her father with confidence. Despite knowing that her father would not support her, she still tries her luck.

Upon approaching her father, she is nervous and insistent that she will be given the fund needed for registration. She started by emphasizing to her father the importance of attending summer camp.

Her father immediately declined to give her the help she needed. Instead, a tray of salted red eggs was presented to her by her father to be sold.

There are around ten trays of salted red eggs available for sale. "Sell these salty red eggs," said her father. Standing there without words, she stared into a blank space.

How would a 17-year-old teenager react? Samantha doesn't know what to feel. Consequently, she thanked her father for allowing her to attend summer camp, and for the salted red eggs.

She immediately searched for a buyer by moving from one store to another on a hot, sunny day since she was insistent on attending summer camp. Luckily, one store took all the eggs, and she sold them all.

She was surprised to find that the amount of money needed for summer camp was more than enough. A valuable lesson she quickly learned was that hard-earned money has value and that being an entrepreneur is worthwhile.

That unique experience further shaped her personality.

During Summer Camp, she discovered her hidden potential and made a lot of life-changing discoveries. She was one of the most outstanding campers. In addition, she won the most valuable player award in the volleyball tournament. She gained many friends, and from then on, her life changes for the better.

As a result, she became a student leader the following school year. It was through this that she was able to inspire many to discover their potential and become a better version of themselves.

Samantha would have missed the opportunity to be coached and trained on how to be a leader if she didn't strive to achieve something.

The ability to aim high can lead to better outcomes, regardless of how large or small the goal may be.

Whenever you embark on an endeavor, you need to be prepared. It takes years for a mango tree to bear fruit. Several forces will hinder the tree's development throughout that period, including droughts, rains, strong winds, wild animals, and many others.

This is how it gets its foundation. After the tree overcomes all obstacles, it will grow big and become fruitful.

About achieving your goals, there are times when you will experience tiredness, boredom, setbacks, discouragement, defeats, etc.

Similarly, a mango tree must overcome many challenges before it becomes a strong and fruitful tree.

As you strive to achieve your goals, you need to overcome all those oppositions ahead. Don't be afraid to accept challenges with an open mind, knowing that no matter what happens, you can overcome them.

PERSONAL APPLICATION/REFLECTION:

5.1   What is your biggest aspiration in life?

____

____

____

____

5.2   Would you prefer to collaborate to achieve it?

____

____

____

____

5.3   When do you plan to start doing it?

____

____

____

____

5.4   What hindrances could occur along the way? How will you solve it?

____

____

____

____

"Those people you admire for their admirable traits can change your perception. It is most likely that you are influenced by these people most of the time"

TOPIC 6

NOBILITY

"There is nothing noble in being superior to your fellow men. True nobility lies in being superior to your former self"

– Hemingway, E.

Having fine and admirable traits can take you further in life. It is not always about the title that makes a person noble. Noblesse oblige is more about a person's characteristics, intentions, and the oddity of being virtuous. It's undeniable that positive attributes are better than intelligence alone.

Others tend to influence individuals by how they relate to them, not by how they make them feel about them (above others). More often than not, people focus only on their own stories, and neglect other people's stories. How they became the person they are now.

Listening to other people's stories lets you escape from your own reality. By doing so, you will gain a better understanding of their perspective and be able to witness the emergence of their noble character.

One of the most astonishing stories about a person with a noble character was the story of Harriet Tubman. She was born into slavery, but known as "the Moses of her people", Harriet was enslaved, escaped, and helped others gain freedom. She pretends to be the underground railroad conductor during the civil war.

She also served as a scout, spy, guerrilla soldier during those times. She has rescued around 70 people on 13 missions. Despite the danger to her life, she chose to help slaves escape.

Harriet has all the reasons in the world to prioritize herself. She can choose to turn a blind eye to the mistreatment of her fellow slaves. She can just walk away. Harriet, however, possesses a noble character. That despite the possibility of being caught, didn't stop her. She continued her rescue mission until she succeeded.

There are individuals who have observed their family members, friends, and colleagues trapped in dysfunctional habits and damaging relationships. However, they still did not dare to intervene.

Caring for people can be extremely risky, particularly if it involves our well-being or avoiding conflict by staying silent in a chaotic environment.

Sometimes, rescue means getting involved. It would take courage to redirect them to the right path.

As Harriet did, adversity didn't stop her. She continued her mission to rescue more slaves.

Harriet's mentality and heart must be emulated. Being brave and capable of helping someone is a noble virtue.

Finally, having a noble character is something you should aspire to have and strive to acquire.

PERSONAL APPLICATION/REFLECTION:

6.1   What good qualities do you possess?

____

____

____

____

6.2   How you will influence others to have these good qualities?

____

____

____

____

6.3   What great qualities do you want to develop that will create an impact on a better society as a whole?

____

____

____

____

"The Key is not to PRIORITIZE What's on your SCHEDULE, But to SCHEDULE your Prioritise"

– Covey S.

TOPIC 7

CAPABILITY

"Ability is what you're capable of doing. Motivation determines what you do. Attitude determines how well you do it"

– Holtz, L.

Now that you have discovered your inner strength, admirable qualities, and characteristics, you are now capable of making your dream a reality.

What's your vision? How do you see yourself 5, or 10 years from now? Activate your desire to accomplish what you envision. Who will be your support system?

When do you want it to happen and how are you going to achieve it? **Invest your inner strength in achieving your goal.** Accept what you cannot and what YOU CAN do. In this manner, you will be able to activate your lifeline. Samantha worked daily to achieve her dreams when she started working on her dreams.

She didn't ignore her daily commitment to achieving her goals. Similar to what you are trying to accomplish, consistency is important to accomplish smaller and more ambitious goals. Though challenges may arise along the way, it is okay. Behold and be BOLD.

As adults, you need to learn to categorize your challenges; things that are out of your control, such as the weather, how people perceive you, and other circumstances.

You place a greater emphasis on things you can control and decide to move forward regardless of that. It is your responsibility to acquire the knowledge necessary to be capable of the things you strive to achieve.

Take a moment to observe your surroundings. Engage yourself in community building and find a group of like-minded people to grow with. There are many organizations where you can find people with the same passion; such as professional organizations or NGOs with the vision to help others.

In Samantha's story, she engaged herself in Toastmasters International, where her communication skills were improved. As part of her journey to develop her public speaking skills, the program where she got involved has been extremely beneficial to her.

Additionally, she volunteers as an assistant to her seasoned professors during presentations, handling technologies like PowerPoint and other videos. She experienced this while studying for her master's degree. For you to constantly train your mindset to be capable of doing either smaller things or more significant things, you have to consistently do it daily. Taking the time to complete a small task daily.

"The key is not to prioritize what's on your schedule, but to schedule your priorities."

– Covey, S.

Getting your goals accomplished by completing your simple daily tasks is the same as completing complicated tasks. This is a simple representation of how small actions you do daily can have a huge impact on the future. Ultimately, being capable of something begins with consistently achieving your priorities daily without hesitation. Such as preparing in advance and setting aside the necessary time to achieve the desired result and that would make you more capable.

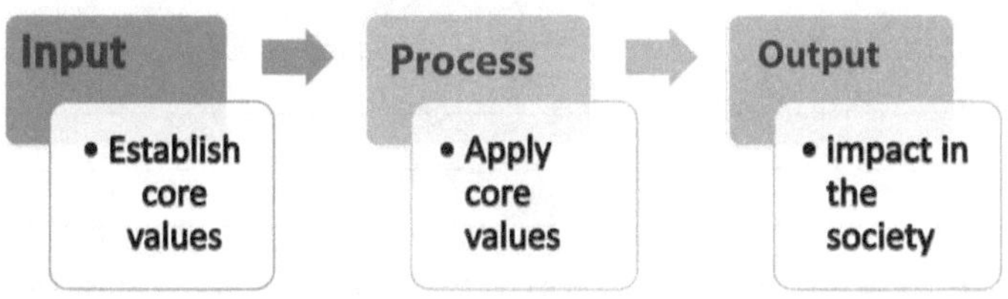

Vision (Framework)

PERSONAL APPLICATION/REFLECTION:

7.1   Write your vision.

____

____

____

____

7.2   What do you see yourself doing five or ten years
      from now?

____

____

____

____

7.3   How is our society you think? 5 or 10 years from now?

____

____

____

____

7.4   Would you be able to contribute to assisting our
      young people in discovering their potential?

____

____

____

____

"The key is not to prioritize what's on your schedule, but to schedule your priorities."

– Covey, S.

Master your inner strength. You can do this by maximizing your daily routine. Embed discipline in your endeavors.

– Mjae D.

TOPIC 8

EMPOWERED TO CONQUER

"A truly empowered person uplifts and adds value to the lives of other people, beginning with himself, his family, and society"

– Unknown

A powerful word to live by. Truly now you are empowered! You have gone through many realizations and reflections.

This time, you have mastered your inner strength. You believe that you can do tremendous things that will alleviate yourself and in turn your family, and society as a whole. Embarked on this new journey, joyously, capturing every possibility to share your skills and talents.

Master your inner strength. You can do this by maximizing your daily routine. Embed discipline in your endeavors.

Chase progress, never settle for mediocrity. Count your daily activities equally important.

Be Objective, and view the situation accordingly. When making a decision, be sure to do it tangibly. Human emotion is powerful; however, you can master it. By doing so, you are becoming detached from being subjective.

Welcome challenges with an open mindset. As the saying goes, only dead people don't experience setbacks. As you progress, remember that there's no such thing as smooth sailing. Like pearls, you are squeezed and experience friction, thus, this is part of the process to emerge victorious.

Try your best to maintain being emancipate from your selfish desire. Be assured that becoming a just person, will surely be in your favor because we know that what comes around goes around.

One of the most powerful speeches was captured during President Lincoln's inaugural address. Lincoln warned the South that he would "have an honorable one to safeguard, protect, and defend it." These are the words coming from an empowered man. "In your hands, my dissatisfied fellow countrymen, and not in mine, is the momentous issue of civil war. The government will not attack you. There is no oath sworn in heaven to destroy the government".

Abraham Lincoln was the 16th President of the United States of America. Lincoln is known primarily for his leadership during the American Civil War and for signing the Emancipation Proclamation, an executive order changing the legal status of slaves to "FREE".

One of his admirable actions while in power was to free slaves. What makes him so powerful is that Lincoln did not have a degree despite becoming a successful lawyer. His total schooling, obtained from traveling teachers, is estimated to be around a year. He was a self-educated man. During his time, Uncle Google was not yet available.

He was the first bearded US President, the first to hold a patent, and the first to be in an inaugural photograph. These are just some of Lincoln's successful stories during his time as a president. Unfortunately, he was assassinated after being president for over 5 years.

His leadership could have brought about more changes. One of his famous quotes that touched many people was "I am a slow walker, but I never walk back."

Being empowered from within can eliminate the spirit of fear, and instead, it can fuel courage, hope, and determination. It is always powerful to believe that we can achieve something; this is a quality we should all strive for.

Raise the bar! Don't be afraid to step up to a higher level. Go and elevate your goals. Developing one set of skills leads to the development of another.

Learning should be lifelong. Enjoy every step of the way. Finally, make a declaration that whatever you do, God will direct you!

PERSONAL APPLICATION/REFLECTION:

8.1   What obstacles you want to conquer.

____

____

____

____

8.2   How you will tackle it?

____

____

____

____

8.3   What is your biggest dream?

____

____

____

____

8.4   How you will achieve your goal/s?

____

____

____

____

TOPIC 9

CRAFTING 100 DREAMS

"it's the possibility of having a dream come true that makes life interesting"

– Paulo Coelho

Now is the time to write down your 100 dreams.

These dreams can become a reality if you put in the effort, such as traveling to another country, learning about a new culture, or just simply eating food from another region.

On top of that, you might meet your favorite author, or leader, after completing a course/program.

What's more, it can be a skill that you want to learn, such as playing guitar or piano. It can also be learning foreign language/s, for example, Filipino, Chinese, Korean, etc. It can also be learning how to use some technological tools, like Adobe illustrator, photoshop, video editing tools, etc. Anything that you want to accomplish such as writing a fictional book, or a novel.

Perhaps you want to create a video channel on YouTube, Facebook, or TikTok.

Also, something that would take time to achieve, for example, getting married, having kids, being a leader in society, or entering public administration. So many things you can dream of. What matters now is writing them down, and completing them one by one.

You may categorize your dreams as follows:

1- 10 – Skills to Learn

11- 20 – Dream Place to Visit

21- 30 - Professional Development

31–40 - Community Involvement

41 - 50 - Meeting your Heroes/Speakers

51 - 60 - Entrepreneurial Activities (investing)

61 - 70 – Competitions/Tournament

71 - 80 - Charitable Works (run for a cause etc.)

81 - 90 – Learn New Languages

91- 100 - Your Long-term goal/s

MY 100 DREAMS

*Skills to Learn

1.____

2.____

3.____

4.____

5.____

6.____

7.____

8.____

9.____

10.____

*Dream Place to Visit

11.____

12.____

13.____

14.____

15.____

16.____

17.____

18.____

19.____

20.____

*Professional Development

21.____

22.____

23.____

24.____

25.____

26.____

27.____

28.____

29.____

30.____

*Community Involvement

31.____

32.____

33.____

34.____

35.____

36.____

37.____

38.______________________________________

39.______________________________________

40.______________________________________

*Meeting your Heroes/ Speakers

41.______________________________________

42.______________________________________

43.______________________________________

44.______________________________________

45.______________________________________

46.______________________________________

47.______________________________________

48.______________________________________

49.______________________________________

50.______________________________________

* Entrepreneurial Activities (investing)

51.______________________________________

52.______________________________________

53.______________________________________

54.______________________________________

55.______________________________________

56.______________________________________

57.______________________________________

58.______________________________________

59.____

60.____

* Competitions/Tournament

61.____

62.____

63.____

64.____

65.____

66.____

67.____

68.____

69.____

70.____

*Charitable Works (run for a cause etc.)

71.____

72.____

73.____

74.____

75.____

76.____

77.____

78.____

79.____

80.____

*Learn New Languages

81.____
82.____

83.____

84.____

85.____

86.____

87.____

88.____

89.____

90.____

*Your Long-term goal/s

91.____

92.____

93.____

94.____

95.____

96.____

97.____

98.____

99.____

100.____

Congratulations! you have identified your 100 dreams.

Now let's make it happen!

Your goal/s are meaningful to me, and I wish you much success in achieving them!

REFERENCES

1. https://www.azquotes.com/quote/661993

2. https://www.brainyquote.com/quotes/ralph_waldo_emerson_387459

3. https://stylesanguine.weebly.com/personality-types.html

4. https://quotefancy.com/quote/1460063/Denzel-Washington-Don-t-aspire-to-make-a-living-aspire-to-make-a-difference

5. https://www.azquotes.com/quotes/topics/capable.html

6. National Geographic Channel, Learn With Us RESOURCE LIBRARY

7. https://www.natgeotv.com

8. https://www.womenshistory.org/education-resources/biographies/harriet-tubman

9. https://www.history.com/topics/us-presidents/abraham-lincoln

Cover Photo Credits: @keendelosa

CONNECT WITH ME

Let's collaborate and engage:

Email: mjaetalks@tutanota.com

Facebook: https://www.facebook.com/mjae.dureza

Instagram: https://www.instagram.com/mjaetalks/

LinkedIn: https://www.linkedin.com/in/mjaedureza/

Tiktok: https://www.tiktok.com/@mjaetalks

YouTube: https://www.youtube.com/@mjaetalks

NOTES